D1367633

LORD, WHY DO THEY ALWAYS WANT HOT DOGS?

by

Dotsey Welliver

Light and Life Press
Winona Lake, Indiana 46590

Copyright © 1977 by
Light and Life Press

All rights reserved. No part of this book may be reproduced in any form,
except for brief quotations in reviews, without the written permission of the
publisher.

ISBN: 0-89367-004-9

Printed in the United States of America by
Light and Life Press
Winona Lake, Indiana
46590

For Mary S.,
who cared

Contents

Introduction

This book had its beginnings several years ago when I participated in turn offering morning devotionals for a faculty prayer meeting. Good friends there, Phil, Mary Alice, and others, kept saying, "You know, you really should write that down."

With their encouragement, I started writing words down. With some of those thoughts expanded and from many experiences later as homemaker and mother of three little scrappers, this collection of chapters, like Topsy, just grew and grew.

This proves a number of points. First, friends reach out and influence each others' lives more than they would ever imagine. Second, when some people begin putting words down, you can hardly stop them. Third, as long as three little boys run in and out, it will take me twice as long to get the words on paper. Finally, and most important, God is very good to give both the words and all the experiences that gave rise to them.

I trust this book will prove one other thing — that the experiences of one ordinary person can be a blessing to others.

Dotsey

FISHHOOKS AND FOOTSTOOLS

Chapter One

Despite my big feet and somewhat horsey laugh, I am irrefragably woman. I loathe dirt and dripping blood. I am afraid of bugs, dogs, and snakes. Collecting a hundred race-car bubble-gum cards is definitely not my idea of a hobby. And football will forever remain pure torture to my nonviolent mind.

God knew all these things. So to prevent my life from becoming pale and listless, He sent three sons into our home. God and I have discussed this way of life many times. I have suggested that, since I have tried to be such a good sport about the invasion of three little boys, He could at least send me a little fame as a sideline. Thus far, I have become the only mother on the block who can belly flop a sled all the way down the steep hill in our alley without knocking over a garbage can.

Considering the remote possibility that I might not yet be ready for world recognition, I have asked Him to at least grant me a rewarding life. Thus far, my rewards have consisted of such things as a bicycle for Christmas (much more useful than a pretty dress) and a kindergarten drawing of a five-hundred-pound, baldheaded woman labeled "My Mommy."

I have asked God for fulfillment. Now follow me through some average days last summer and see how full I really am.

A knock on the door. "Can Daniel come out to play?" The face of Daniel's little six-year-old friend smiled sweetly up at me. I knew what lurked behind all the freckles. I have known plenty of his kind. A few days before, in the space of one hour, he had set fire to our lawn and had plastered my two-year-old from head to foot with mud. (I cannot and will not deny that my two-year-old aided and abetted the entire situation and expressed satisfaction with the results.)

The center of gravity for little boys ages two through twelve sometimes seems to be at my front door. Young males of many different varieties keep dropping in from all over.

One day I counted five knocks at the door while I was trying to give a piano lesson. One toilet stop. Two drinks of water. One "What time is it? Mommy said send me home at eleven." And one "Can we bury a dead bird in your yard?"

Now back to my little friend at the door. I stood weighing my decision carefully. On the one hand, there was the possibility of getting Daniel out of the house for a while. On the other hand, what were Daniel's possibilities of surviving?

I looked down again into that upturned face, and You spoke to me, Father. Now that I think about it, You have often spoken to me through a child. A sentence flashed through my mind. I had read the words in a book somewhere long ago. "To love is a full-time divine employment." Now there is an occupation worthy of the name — one which holds out the promise of much lasting fulfillment. Before signing on, however, I have some questions:

1. Must I love this little guy even while the grass is burning?
2. How many drinks of water must I love a child through?
3. How many broken windows and trampled tomato plants must I forgive?
4. How many little boys must I find the time to love?

Your Holy Spirit is a wonderful teacher, Father; and the answers came quick and fast.

1. Yes, even while the grass is burning. Little boys are far more important than grass.
2. Matthew 10:42. "And whosoever shall give to drink unto one of these little ones a cup of cold water ... he shall in no wise lose his reward."
3. Matthew 18:21-22. "Then came Peter to him, and said, Lord, how oft shall my brother sin against me, and I forgive him? ... Jesus saith unto him, I say ... unto thee, ... Until seventy times seven."
4. You must love every little boy Christ died for.

Ah, yes, forgive me, Father. Sometimes when

chaos reigns, my vision dims. Thank You for reminding me that loving these ferocious, bellowing little souls will bear results through eternity. Besides that, having a friend with two teeth missing in front is far more rewarding than having a well-manicured lawn.

Yes, now I see that fulfillment can come through having a yard disreputable enough to serve as a bird cemetery.

Satisfaction can surely come from baking a birthday cake in the form of a giraffe. (I say it was a pretty good giraffe, and I felt very artistic and worthwhile. I can't help it that the boys thought it was a rabbit.)

Boring days certainly do not come often as long as You send me little boys to love and serve. And liberation becomes meaningful any day when I have freely chosen to do Your will. Yes, the job sounds challenging enough. When I punch in on Your time clock, Master, please help me be able to mark each day up to loving service.

There were other days equally rewarding, some with more fulfillment than I actually ever asked for.

There was fishing-down-at-the-creek day. I found meaning then by learning a new skill. Following emergency instructions from the doctor over the phone, I soon caught on to the neat little trick involved in removing a fishhook from a small boy's finger.

There were a number of you-know-good-and-well-you-punched-me-first days when sibling rivalry nearly brought about mass homicide. I achieved a real sense of confidence on those days in my knowledge of child psychology. I threatened to pound the daylights out of the first kid who opened his mouth again, after which I felt very liberated, although the boys did not.

Then there was the vacuum-finally-whooshed-its-last day. It had been coughing and groaning for some time. It then inhaled violently and went up in smoke.

Yes, days like these are a familiar part of a woman's world. Who needs it? I do! For now I am also remembering other days that had meaning.

I recall the excitement before Christmas over the secret project in the works out in the garage. After much hammering and whispered consultations in private, my eight-year-old presented me with a bright red footstool. Footstools that love makes simply do not need to match the other furniture, and he knows I love red. You may prefer the seventy-five-dollar model at Macy's, but I do not. Give me a bright red, slightly wobbly one any time.

Then there was Valentine's Day. After much adding of pennies, my three-man band-aid brigade showed up with a green headscarf for me. Now there was a very good reason for knowing that I needed a headscarf. They had played with my black one in the car and had let it blow out the window. Nevertheless, a green headscarf bought with Cupid's money is far preferable to a black one any day.

Less special occasions have their high points

as well. Like the day my fourth-grader came home from school and announced, "I told every kid in the class today that you are our room-mother this year." After I had quelled a few riots at the Halloween party, his classmates were a little impressed. He, however, continued to swell with pride.

My Father, I praise You for Your very real presence in my life. You do not dwell on some remote, inaccessible mountain. I have found You to be near while milk oozed all over my clean floor. You have filled me with peace through seemingly interminable Pee Wee League ball games. You have given me joy in the middle of the night while I was singing "Jesus Loves Me" for the seventeenth time to quiet a scared baby. You have given me strength and calm while I was driving to the hospital emergency room with a little boy spitting out teeth and blood all along the way.

I thank You for being God over broken vacuums, fishhooks, and Little League. I can even believe You like red footstools. I praise You for giving meaning to my woman's world!

SWEET
RUNNING
CHEVY

Chapter Two

I am a devoted fan of Norman Rockwell's paintings. I was looking through some prints the other day and noticed his series on freedoms — Freedom from Want, Freedom from Fear, Freedom of Speech, and Freedom of Worship. As I thought on the meanings of these freedoms for our country, I realized also that the first three represent sound reasons for marriage.

Yes, marriage offers me freedom from want. I am not lacking companionship. I am not lacking communication. Aloneness is fine in small doses, but over the long haul I prefer to have someone around to talk to — in good times and bad. I like having someone around who loves me and who tells me so. Inside the free life-styles of many young couples today, companionship and love may be here today and gone tomorrow. I like a more permanent and trustworthy arrangement according to God's plan.

Marriage also offers me freedom from financial want — if I don't want too much! I appreciate a husband who works steadily and willingly to provide for his family.

This leaves me free to put my home first. This leaves me free to develop my own life-style and talents without being bound to outside employment. This leaves me free to be the organizer of my own time. This allows me more time for spiritual development — in short, more time to be me and to consider what God wants for me.

Marriage also offers me freedom from certain fears — the fear of being rejected and a fear of being compared with others. I consider it a great blessing to belong to one man, and he to me. I never suffer comparisons with other women, for he wants no other. And this same freedom from comparison is true on both sides. We need not worry about being rejected for someone else younger, richer, or more beautiful. This fact also frees me to be myself and to find the unique place God has for me in this world.

Marriage offers me freedom of speech. There are certain things I can say to him that I would not dare to say to anyone else. I can be sure he will love me anyway. He knows me well enough that I cannot shock him anymore. I am free to express my inner thoughts if I so desire. I would never feel such freedom to share deeply inside any less permanent relationship.

We can often find out what something means to us by looking at what it is not.

Marriage at my house is not surprise gifts of flowers. We are more likely to have toy cars sitting in the middle of the table.

Marriage is not a romantic ocean voyage.

Instead we go to tractor pulls. He goes for interest's sake. I go to be with him.

For us marriage is not simply an arrangement which provides a steady escort for a long series of social affairs. A night out on the town is rare enough to be really exciting.

Marriage offers many positive things to me. Marriage is:

Adult conversation at the end of the day

Riding in a pickup truck

Someone to pick up the prescription when I am sick

Someone to laugh with

A warm bed

Having someone to help decide how to handle a stubborn, naughty little boy

Someone to try out all my ridiculous ideas on

Strong hands to open the catsup bottle

Having someone along who knows east from west

Someone to trust

Someone to be comfortable with

You may have guessed by now. Our marriage does not resemble a Cadillac limousine so much as it does a trusty and comfortable Chevrolet sedan. However, we have motored along quite happily together for some thirteen years.

We like what we've got.

Father, thank You for the joy and, yes, the responsibility of sharing another person's life. Help us to touch and influence and help build each other's lives into temples bringing glory to You.

"LOOK, NO HANDS!"

Chapter Three

Men and masculinity? Since I have now spent some 113,952 woman-hours cohabiting a home with a husband and three sons, I feel somewhat qualified to speak on such a subject. I am particularly acquainted with males of the two-to-twelve-year-old variety.

These things I know.

Little boys have ears that stand in danger of dissolving if they come within ten feet of a washcloth.

Boys wiggle their way through Sunday school and church.

Boys are terribly concerned with becoming strong. The Bible story of Samson is usually one of their favorites.

Boys love riddles and knock-knock jokes. They can riddle you into a coma faster than bullets.

If a sidewalk and a series of mudholes border on the same street, boys will invariably choose to walk home through the mudholes. The sidewalk is only for crawling on with new pants.

Little boys keep our clothing economy moving. Pockets fall off their shirts at the slightest provocation. Knees in blue jeans simply disintegrate. Their shoes often seem to be made of tissue paper.

Boys (large and small) are the great benefactors of companies that manufacture car and airplane models.

If you spend two hours preparing chicken tetrazzini for dinner, little boys will ask why we can't have hot dogs.

Boys can ask more questions than all the encyclopedias in the world can answer.

"How big is a giant's baby?"

"How can I make some gunpowder?"

"How many worms can a person eat before he gets sick?"

From very noisy, boisterous beginnings, boys grow up into important destinies.

The wild Indians now racing through your flower beds may someday sit on a judge's bench, deciding cases that will influence an entire community or nation.

That little guy with two scratches and a purple knot on his head may some day be your pastor.

That small male bicycling wildly down the street and yelling, "Look, no hands!" may someday be manufacturing the automobile which can be driven "no hands" — guided by electronic cables buried in the street.

That grimy little urchin now pilfering the toolbox may one day be your plumber, mechanic, trashman — or, most startling of all (with those greasy hands), your surgeon.

The Lord God himself said in Ezekiel 22:30, "And I sought for a man among them, that should make up the hedge, and stand in the gap before me . . . ."

And where indeed, shall we find this man? Well, of course, at age ten we shall find him up a tree, or in a ditch, or on a bicycle, or playing ball, or fighting enthusiastically with a sibling.

But when our boys have become men, please, God, may we find them filling gaps for You.

HIGH HEELS
AND
DOLLIES

Chapter Four

Since my writing nearly always involves boys, some readers may accuse me of slighting little girls. Not for one moment do I ignore girls, for running around right now somewhere in a little girl's world are the future mothers of my grandchildren.

However, I do not myself have little girls, and I only faintly remember being one. But since all sorts of people these days are expounding on subjects about which they know next to nothing, I feel justified here in telling all I barely know about young females.

In years of teaching elementary school, working with children in various church activities, and teaching private piano lessons, I have noted a few differences between girls and boys.

Little girls seem to do more bouncing around. Boys do more shuffling, jumping, and exploding.

Little girls are less predictable. From my observation, girls can easily switch in ten seconds from "piano" to "fortissimo" in either music or emotions. Boys generally can be expected to maintain a steady, strong, reputable "fortissimo."

Little girls write notes with butterflies and flowers colored all over, saying "I love teacher." Boys write notes with race cars, reading "Grils [sic] stink."

A girl will normally wear an orange- and gold-checkered blouse with orange pants and a purple and white blouse with purple pants. Boys are much more likely to wear an orange and gold shirt with purple pants, and a purple and white shirt with orange pants.

Girls get vaporous and breathless over a piano recital. Boys get a near-fatal form of paralysis if they come within two miles of a recital.

Little girls love to attend wedding receptions. Boys scratch and pick their noses at such gatherings.

Girls seem to giggle a lot. Girls are also very gifted with speech. In past months I have paid close attention to the conversation of my piano students as they come and go. The girls often mention school parties and decorations, Grandma's visit, their sweet little pet kitty, staying overnight with a friend, or a shopping trip with Mother. Boys mutter a sparse sentence or two, maybe something like, "Is El Goofo still taking lessons?" or "How long can thirty minutes last, anyway?"

Little girls are fussy and neat about many things, except possibly the condition of their own rooms (so I am told).

Boys are fastidious about almost nothing, except possibly a younger brother who keeps "breaking up the joint."

Girls are toy stoves and dishes, Mommy's high heels, a favorite doll, and little lamb barrettes.

Boys are a racing-car set, electric football, a favorite Scout knife, and an unwindable cowlick.

My life has been enriched by my contacts with little girls, and I thank God for them.

God's highest gift to Adam was a female. Adam may not have known quite what to do with her, but God knows what to do with girls.

God calls them to bear and train the next generation of citizens. They are placed in positions to teach spiritual values and wield great influence over our future poets and preachers and philosophers and presidents. (In these days, they may even become the same.)

The book of Proverbs sets the price of a good woman far above rubies. In these days of inflation, that represents a great fortune, indeed.

God, help our girls to know their strengths and use them wisely. May their powerful influence always be used for Your work in our world. We thank You for their beauty, their grace, and their love.

LONG LIVE BIRTHDAYS!

Chapter Five

I may have set some kind of endurance record. I just took nine junior-age boys into the city for a special matinee in honor of my oldest son's birthday. We made the thirty-mile round trip (nine boys plus my own substantial poundage) in a small '63 Studebaker dubbed the Green Hornet. The Studebaker had already traveled 156,000 miles — but never before had the little automobile seen such spectacular miles.

The boys dared me with great huzzahs to race every car that hove into sight. No matter that the Green Hornet was loaded to the shocks. No matter that the other car was a shiny '75 model with only one person in it. When I finally did manage to pass one small grandma, fastidiously observing thirty miles an hour, pandemonium broke loose.

Not only did the boys want to race; they also wanted to argue. First, they nearly had fisticuffs over their fathers' former military ranks. The only thing I know is that a man with a bird on his shoulder is somebody important, so I refused to referee. After the fact had been established that at least four boys (the four loudest ones) had fathers who were generals, they moved on to something more interesting.

Once they ran out of anything to argue about, and for ten seconds silence reigned supreme. Their nervous systems could not endure the quiet, of course, so they took a vote on whether they should start arguing again. The vote was unanimous. Vociferous disputing was definitely their favorite sport. So someone brought up the track average of some famous miler, and their convivial good spirits resumed until we reached our destination.

I have just finished telling you about the dull part of the trip. Now we come to the dramatic moments.

Some unwritten law is apparently in effect forbidding the purchasing, all at the same time, of a candy bar, a Coke, a bag of popcorn, an ice-cream bar, and a pack of chewing gum from a refreshment stand. Thus, each item had to be bought separately. We averaged four trips per boy to the snack bar.

The problems in the little boys' room will not bear telling. Suffice it to say, some 250-pound man finally threatened to beat their noses in unless they all cleared the area in five seconds flat. Leggy little boys came bounding out of the rest room door in all directions, like gazelles fleeing a forest fire. I wanted to hang around and commend the man when he came out, but I was afraid of what he might do to me for bringing on such a plague.

Another man watched us from the sidewalk as we were leaving. I had difficulty getting all nine boys into the car at the same time. When they were finally inside, I could not get the noses to stay still long enough to be counted. The man shook his head with resignation as he turned to leave. "How much is it worth to you, ma'am?" he said. "How much is an afternoon like this worth to you?"

A good question. And I think it deserves an answer.

Here's what it's worth.

The Bible assures us that a human soul is worth more than all the worldly material things put together. Just one human soul. I assume, then, that the chance to influence a human personality would indeed be a great opportunity. I had nine such opportunities at once that afternoon.

Jesus was willing to die for those nine little boys. If He loved them so much, surely I can find them worthwhile. And each unique personality is indeed a treasure.

The afternoon was also worth a lot of memories — some bittersweet, to be sure. But of such days is nostalgia made.

In fact, one little boy was worth it all. My son thought the day perfect in all respects and voiced his opinion later as I lay on the couch in a state of near-exhaustion. "Man, Mom, that was the superest birthday of my whole life!"

Yes, human lives are worth it — worth all the effort, worth the time, worth investing our energies in. I believe that every human life is a fresh and unique personality come from God, into our world. I respect the potential of each little boy (and girl). Each birthday reestablishes the fact that God thinks each of us is worth something individually.

Long live birthdays!

Long live little boys!

Long live their mothers' endurance!

Thank You, Lord, for all our special days, and the non-special days as well. The assurance of Your presence can easily make my day sacred. I praise You, too, for all the people who fill our days – sometimes with challenge, occasionally conflict, and often comfort. Considering Calvary, I know all these persons are important to You. Help me never forget that fact.

CALL
HIM
CHEERFUL

Chapter Six

One of the most delightful and thought-consuming tasks an expectant mother has is in choosing a name for her little one. This can also be a very frustrating chore, especially if the husband and wife disagree on basic types of names.

In our family (and not having daughters, I cannot speak with authority concerning girl names) I like less common names, brisk and full of masculinity, like Kent, Dane, or Colby. Doug likes the old no-nonsense standbys like John, Ronald, and Charles. We were so taken up with defending our positions regarding names that we generally forgot to consider the meaning of the names.

And names are important. Our three-year-old just now is beginning to learn to recognize his name when it is printed on paper. A paper with those precious letters DAYLON on it is worth more to him than gold. He has several such sheets of paper strewn around his room right now.

Our Heavenly Father considers names important. He made Adam responsible for giving each animal a name (Genesis 2:19). He even calls the stars by name (Psalm 147:4). If He cared so much for the beasts of the field and starry heavens, we may be sure He cares about our names. "And he calleth his own sheep by name, and leadeth them out" (John 10:3).

God changed the names of people to fit new personalities: for example, Abram, Sarai, Jacob, Saul, and Simon. And, oh, wonder of wonders, they became what he named them. Jacob became Israel, prince of God, and Simon became Peter the Rock.

I have been wondering whether we mothers should learn a lesson from this.

I once called a child Grouchy, and I affirmed this name over and over till he could not help but live up to it. Then one day, the Lord helped me see what I was doing. I began to compliment him on the times few and far between when he was actually Cheerful or even Slightly Less than Grouchy. I was never really able to think of him as Sunshine, which, when you think about it, would be pretty hard for anyone to measure up to constantly. However, to my utter amazement, more and more he would live up to what I expected of his personality. He became Pleasant, Delightfully Witty, and even occasionally Enthusiastic. And you may now call me Thankful.

I am intrigued by Revelation 2:17: "To him

that overcometh will I give to eat the hidden manna, and will give him a white stone, and in the stone a new name written, which no man knoweth saving he that receiveth it."

Yes, it seems that you and I and all our children have names known only to God. He is already affirming what He knows we can be. Will I be known as Faithful, or Prayerful, or Merciful? Are you known to God as Praising? Forgiving? Or Patience?

I believe we as mothers can help further God's work on this earth by giving our children names that will testify to all the possibilities they have through the power of the Lord Jesus Christ in their lives.

Let us name our indifferent scholars Achievers. And keep encouraging and praising and affirming every decent achievement.

Let us rename our selfish ones Compassion and compliment every shred of love and sharing that can be found, not missing one opportunity to offer encouragement.

Let us rename our belligerent ones Peaceful until we see the peacemakers actually becoming the children of God.

We might even take the totally drastic step of renaming our husbands. Do we dare affirm them as Compassion, Sensitive, Courageous? Shall we name them Wonderful, and Loyal, and Spiritual Achievers?

Dear God, help us all to have names that meet with Your approval.

VIEW FROM A TREASURE CHEST

Chapter Seven

Determined to get a fresh glimpse of the true spirit of praise one year, I covenanted with myself to remain alert during one day to each little blessing that made my heart sing.

So I sat down to see how many of those memories I could record in one hour. At the end of the hour, I was rather disappointed to discover that I had recorded only nine specific blessings. I sat up astounded, however, when I decided to see how many definite blessings I could have counted in my lifetime at that rate. Figuring sixteen waking hours a day, you can perhaps imagine my amazement when I discovered that I could have already counted 1,516,320 glorious treasures in my lifetime.

I would like to share those nine recorded blessings with you in the hope that you, too, will look around and realize anew that "the blessing of the Lord, it maketh rich."

*　　*　　*

Thank You, Father, that I woke up.

Life is cause for celebration!

(I have always tended to meet the dawn in a condition once described aptly by Mark Twain. After being rescued from a near-fatal swimming attempt, he was brought out, he said, in a most limp and unpromising condition.)

To wiggle a toe is at least a minor miracle.

To rise and walk — an affirmation of Your sustaining power.

Thank You for the light, Father.

I flipped a switch, and it flashed forth, dazzling, revealing, brilliant, warm.

A reminder of Your Holy Spirit ... powerful ... illuminating, operating with more kilowatt hours than the world ever dreamed.

And You send no utility bills!

Thank You for my sons ... dynamos ... perpetual motion.

Chugging, pushing, running, screaming,

Poking, laughing, yelling, scheming,

Driving me to a glass of water and aspirin.

Unhappy, unhealthy children do not pulsate so.

Hurrah for seeing, smelling, touching, hearing.

I can see! Dirty dishes ... unironed clothes ... the robin prancing in the tree.

I can smell! The burned toast ... the rose love offered me.

I can hear! I can feel!

Cheers for the butterfly the children chased today.

24

Such fleeting beauty, sweet reminder of those
sparkling, shimmering moments of life
flitting by on wings of gold, so small, yet
remaining in memory forever. An unexpected compliment, maybe, or the unde-
served favor of a friend.

*Thank You, Master, for my freedom ... my
cherished free will.*

Precious gift of God.

The right to be me ...

To choose the kind of person I shall be.

I praise You for the noise.

The swish-swooshing on the freeway ...

the stream of jet traffic overhead ...

the janitor and his brooms clunking.

Now I can appreciate Your stillness ...

Your peace ... Your quiet presence in my
life.

I love the challenge that came my way today.

Golden opportunity to put love in action,

to see Your love transform.

Besides, hard work makes my rest so much
sweeter.

I was thrilled when a little child prayed for me.

"Lord, please bless Mrs. Welliver today."

Thank You, Father, for the love of that child.

Thank You for her soft fawn eyes,

the brunette ringlets dancing a circlet,

her bouncing steps celebrating health,

her trusting heart and bountiful faith.

*And thank You, too, Master, for answering her
prayer.*

DECISIONS, DECISIONS, DECISIONS

Chapter Eight

Lately, I have been feeling much as the young fellow did who quit his job sorting potatoes because the decisions were getting him down.

Life seems to be one long decision-making process.

The flu has come to visit. Through a series of fevers, I must decide whether to take that particular child to the doctor and wreck the family budget or try to tough it out and possibly regret my decision later.

Then the curtains in one bedroom successfully finished their job of deteriorating disgracefully. Should I pay more this time for good quality curtains? Should I risk another pair of cheap ones (which did not prove to be very wise last time)? Should I try to make my own curtains and perhaps display my amazing talent for ruining material? Or shall we simply do without for a while? And perhaps there are still other options which I have not thought of yet. As of this writing, we are still doing without while I ponder the matter further. The boys have never noticed the missing curtains.

Facing the possibility of being buried under a landslide of junk, I decided to clean the closets. The boys immediately became defensive concerning every little possession. We are going through agonizing processes trying to decide what to throw away.

How do I go about making wise decisions? The following questions have helped me formulate a procedure: First, is this decision in line with God's Word? If not, we can toss the whole matter immediately. God's commandments do not lend themselves to moral relativity.

Second, is this indecision on my part a result of my fear of failure? I have often waited far too long making some decision if my reputation for brilliance seemed to be at stake. I must accept the fact that I cannot call all the shots perfectly.

Third, is this indecision wasting more time than the results are worth? God expects me to be a good steward of my talents, possessions, and money. He also expects me to be a wise steward of my time. The hours I waste considering curtains may be more precious from eternity's viewpoint than the slight difference in dollars. Pondering decisions overtime is one of the world's great time robbers.

In considering this matter, am I creating more tension than the wrong decision would? Indecision nearly always brings about an unsettled feeling that fills me with anxiety.

I try not to settle for asking, "Is this a good decision?" Especially on the more major decisions, I ask instead, "Is this the most excellent decision possible? Is this a part of God's very highest and best for my life?"

Is this something that can honestly wait? If I am not wasting too much time worrying about the problem, waiting may be best for now. More information on the subject may come to light later.

I also try to remember that God's options are not numbered. Sometimes when I am at the very point of deciding, He brings up some delightful solution which I had not been able to think of.

Although I do believe that God expects us to use the sound minds and common sense He gave us, I still find it beneficial always to ask His direction. I am amazed at the sometimes great results that accrue from some very small decision in our lives.

I think others must also have problems in making decisions. Some years ago, I was part of a small group taking training in speaking at evangelistic teas. We were busily preparing our testimonies. Out of five women, three used Proverbs 3:5 and 6 as the scripture that had been most helpful to them. These words are, indeed, a precious promise, and I go back to them when some decision hangs heavy over my head. "Trust in the Lord with all thine heart; and lean not unto thine own understanding. In all thy ways acknowledge him, and he shall direct thy paths."

This verse does not say, "in part of thy ways,"

or "occasionally," or "just on the biggies, acknowledge me." The Word plainly states: "in *all* thy ways."

Father, I thank You that I can come to You and talk about flu, and curtains, and which objects to throw away. Knowing that You keep count of the sparrows assures me that I, too, am an object of Your love and concern. When I think of all Your wisdom and the fact that You are willing to share some of it with me, I can face my days of decision with greater confidence and less tension.

MUSCLE POWER

Chapter Nine

Froggy Baby, Omar the Giant, and Don the Body Beautiful were having their nightly wrestling match in my living room.

As I tiptoed to the door to watch, Don the Body Beautiful (my bony adolescent) flexed his almost nonexistent muscles, preened like a peacock, and strutted into the imaginary ring. Froggy Baby (the four-year-old) was already in the ring, poised for action. Omar was the referee for this round.

I cannot remember a time when my boys were not interested in muscle power. By the age of four, each one had started the habit of daily sizing up his muscles. The oldest (who has always been extremely spindly) one day said to me, "Mom, am I the only broad-shouldered one in the family?"

At the age of five in a kindergarten Bible class, this same son made his personal commitment to

Jesus. As is the case with many parents, I watched closely to see whether he understood what he had done. Some weeks later, in a chapel service at the Christian school he attended, they asked the young children to give testimonies. My pride and joy jumped up immediately and with shining face said, "When Jesus came into my heart, He made me feel like the strongest man in the whole world!"

What better proof do we need that Jesus meets each one of us at the point relevant to our own need?

My youngest boy now asks periodically, "Mommy, do you think my muscles are getting any heavier?"

I don't know about his muscles, but mine are definitely getting heavier, and the scales prove it. I have always been the kind to trim my fingernails carefully before stepping on the scales, but still the story is sad. I need a great deal of strength just to carry my muscles around.

When you consider an average week at my house, you will understand my questions about strength. A normal week may well include a day or two of substitute teaching, giving some fifteen private piano lessons, pounding the typewritter for several hours, plus digging out from under who knows what. Three times daily, I must feed four normal people and one bottomless pit. For excitement, a trip into town may be included or perhaps a school party which I must room-mother.

Strength, oh, strength, where can you be

found? How long will you last? To which end shall I use you?

I turned to God's Word to find some answers.

I found only one source of strength: "The Lord is my light and my salvation; whom shall I fear? the Lord is the strength of my life; of whom shall I be afraid?" (Psalm 27:1).

"The Lord will give strength unto his people " (Psalm 29:11).

How long can I trust such strength to hold out? "Trust ye in the Lord for ever: for in the Lord Jehovah is everlasting strength" (Isaiah 26:4).

I also discovered that God supplies our strength day by day. If He granted me a year's supply at once, I am sure I would be tempted to squander it all in the first couple of months. But day by day I can come and receive the full measure for the needs of that day, ". . . and as thy days, so shall thy strength be" (Deuteronomy 33:25).

Am I responsible for being a good steward of my energy? How do I choose the correct way of expending my strength?

"Thou shalt love the Lord thy God with all thy heart, and with all thy soul, and with all thy mind, and with all thy strength: this is the first commandment" (Mark 12:30).

Father, I thank You for the strength to love and serve You through all the days of my life.

LOVE
AND THE
SNACK SHACK

Chapter Ten

How often we pray for some glorious and saintly job to do — some job that will call forth great consecration and holiness. While we are praying thus, the answer in slight disguise stands staring us in the face.

More and more, I have been realizing that the greatest dedication for wives and mothers usually involves a more practical and daily sort of love.

I have not been asked to preside over influential meetings of our city leaders. Instead, I was called this week to work in the Little League Snack Shack. I do not care for this type of service. But love demands that a Christian mother become involved in some way in community life.

I was not asked this week to offer deep theological insights to a gathering of prophets and priests. I *was* called upon to console and advise a child. Some older boys had been throwing walnuts at him. Yes, my son, life does throw its "walnuts" at us all. We learn either to

33

accept them, avoid them, or make friends with the walnut throwers.

I was not sought after for my great healing powers. I did take a child in for his vaccination, however, thereby helping keep diphtheria, tetanus, and whooping cough at bay.

No one has extolled my profound understanding of great spiritual truths for some time now. However, a mother did tell me that her child was enjoying my Sunday school class.

I could not retreat to a monastic cell this week for long hours of contemplation. But I did remember a friend's need while I was ironing. I prayed each morning for God's watch-care over the schoolchildren. And I asked God to give my husband a light and loving heart at work each day.

I had no opportunity to join a citizens' group or march on Washington, D.C. I could *and did* write a letter to our senator involving a matter of Christian stewardship.

I was not visited with any prophetic and sacred visions this week. No whirlwind from the sky announced some great and mighty work to be done. The Holy Spirit did bring to mind several commands from God's Word — all the "mighty work" I could possibly attend to. "Go and teach," "Love one another," "Bear one another's burdens," "Love the Lord thy God with all thy heart."

God demanded no act of martyrdom from me this week — save only this: "And he said to them all, If any man will come after me, let him deny himself, and take up his cross daily, and follow me" (Luke 9:23).

Yes, I think I am beginning to see. A very genuine sort of love may be involved in baking a cake.

When love prompts the action, making party decorations with a child may become a high and holy calling.

Spiritual insights may be as easily discovered while waxing a floor as when reading some great classic.

Time spent listening to a friend may in the end yield results equally as glorious as the most erudite sermon.

Heavenly Father, help me to be able to say with John Wesley:

> I am no longer my own, but thine;
> Put me to what thou wilt;
> Rank me with whom thou wilt;
> Put me to doing, put me to suffering;
> Let me be employed for Thee, or laid aside for Thee;
> Exalted for Thee or brought low for Thee;
> Let me be full; let me be empty;
> Let me have all things, let me have nothing.
> I freely and heartily yield all things to Thy pleasure and disposal.

THE
GRATITUDE
ATTITUDE

Chapter Eleven

Some days are definitely depressing.

A recent birthday serves as a good example. I am rapidly reaching an age when birthdays in themselves can be depressing. However, on this particularly icy day in January, something malfunctioned in our furnace and could not be repaired until my husband came home from work. Since I had shopping to do anyway, I decided to drive into town and stay inside the warm stores until almost time for him to come home.

One block down the street, the car had a flat tire. I climbed out, picked up a sleeping baby, and walked back home to spend the rest of my birthday afternoon inside a freezing house. I could feel the depression growing.

Dr. Tim LaHaye, in his book *How to Win over Depression*, states that in all his years of counseling, he has discovered self-pity to be the factor more than any other which brings about depression. In my own experiences and in sharing with friends, I must agree with him.

The bottom had not fallen out of my world at all. In fact, I had a beautiful opportunity to take an afternoon off, crawl under the electric blanket, and read for several hours. At any other time I would have welcomed the chance. But then, I began to feel sorry for myself.

Who else is ever caught in such a situation? Why does it always have to happen to me? And on my birthday, of all things! Without much effort at all, I conjured up a striking case of depression.

I cannot speak with certainty concerning men, but I believe that women are peculiarly susceptible to this malady of self-pity. Full-time homemakers particularly have to be on the watch. We have more time (around that second cup of coffee, perhaps), after the house has emptied in the mornings, to spend a few moments thinking about all the things that have gone wrong lately.

Authorities are assuring us that depression has become the leading emotional illness in our nation and is rapidly increasing.

I certainly do not claim to have all the authoritative answers. But I have found a few methods that help me.

The first step is definitely to avoid feeling sorry for myself. The best way to do this is to develop a "gratitude attitude." When you find yourself counting up all the sad things, make an even longer list of the good things that have happened recently. If this seems to be very difficult for you, then you know you really need it. Without realizing, you may have become one of those habitual gripers — a morose woman who simply takes delight in wallowing around in an advanced case of self-pity. You must make every effort to crawl out or else face the specter of depression for a large portion of your life.

Another thing that has helped me is learning to pray honestly. God means for us to be victorious Christians, but pretending never makes it so. God accepts no bogus checks. If we are depressed, He already knows it and wants to do something about it. Tell Him specifically what is bothering you. Learn to accept your own part of responsibility for it. Even in cases where depression may be caused by some unavoidable event (such as the loss of a loved one), you may be grieving longer than is good for you or the rest of your family. You may also be indicating a lack of belief in Romans 8:28: "All things work together for good to them that love God."

Another helpful step for me has been expanding my horizons. I can nearly always help myself up out of a depressed state by meeting a need for someone else. Instead of looking inwardly at the problems for a long time, look up and then look outwardly. Someone needs you today in some way. And your service to that person will prove to be a service to yourself.

I also have a very practical little gimmick that has worked many times for me. I make a list of specific projects that I need to be working on and then set a definite time limit for their completion.

A lack of purpose in life can be most depressing. I nearly always have a list of goals. Depression proves to be a good time to go to work on one of them. Not only do I gain a great sense of satisfaction in the achievement of the goal and thereby lose my depression; I also get rid of the sense of guilt over procrastinating.

In overcoming depression, I have accomplished some major goals in developing my own life's message for Jesus Christ.

"Finally, my brethren, be strong in the Lord, and in the power of his might" (Ephesians 6:10).

Lord of all earth and heaven too, Lord of our valleys as well as our mountains, have mercy upon us, encased as we are inside imperfect bodies and emotions. Help us fix our eyes upon You, where there is no shadow of turning. Help us cast our instabilities on the one who can handle them all without wavering. Through happy times and sad, let us be found tightly holding Your hand.

NATIONAL SMILE WEEK

Chapter Twelve

Could I possibly have heard the voice correctly? "National Smile Week!" And at eight o'clock on a Monday morning! I felt like throwing a shoe right through the television screen.

I rushed into the family room to see who could possibly be so cheery. And there they were, my three male progeny, listening intently as Captain Kangaroo announced National Smile Week. It took their fancy immediately. Each one started trying to talk at once with an exaggerated smile. At that hour, I needed some activity slightly less strenuous than smiling, so I retreated.

After about three minutes, their jaws began to numb. Another couple of minutes, and I overheard this very interesting conversation — every word uttered through clenched teeth and a forced, supersized smile.

"You started it, Doug; you know you did. You punched me first."

"Nuh-uh. You know that's not so. You punched me first."

"I did not. You always start it. And anyhow, you know it's not fair to fight during National Smile Week."

"Yes, it is too fair. I can fight all I want to, just as long as I keep smiling."

With jaws numb and lips stretched wide to the bitter end, they lit into each other, tooth and toenail. They did a beautiful job of fulfilling the letter of the law of National Smile Week. However, by a few choice phrases passed back and forth, I perceived they were somewhat less than dedicated in keeping the spirit of that law.

While I was meditating on that little incident, Father, You spoke to me. You reminded me that You have declared every week "National Love Week." Yet, how many times have I as a Christian sallied forth into the world with a brave outsized smile resolving, "I'll do it. I'll love 'em this week even if it kills me." And it nearly does. So I am looking for some answers.

As a psychology major in college, I was interested to note that, while the different writers of the various textbooks disagreed widely as to their methods, they did all agree on one basic fact. With one accord, they stated that the deepest need of the human heart seemed to be love. On that point I need no convincing. I know my own heart all too well.

I had this truth brought home to me in a most forceful way a few years later while teaching in a Christian day school.

My husband was being transferred from California to Kansas, and it had become necessary for me to tell my second-grade friends that I was leaving. Tears began to well up in the eyes of some of the little girls. Some of the boys began jumping up and down with glee.

I then proceeded to tell them about the new teacher and all her qualifications. I emphasized with great enthusiasm her good education and many years of teaching experience. I waxed eloquent concerning her degrees. I stressed the fact that she had children and grandchildren.

When I finished, one of the little fellows was right on the edge of his seat, waving his hand furiously and grunting loudly. (There is at least one like him in every classroom.) He would not be denied. "Yes, Ronald, what is it?"

He very solemnly and earnestly replied, "Well, Mrs. Welliver, what we really want to know is, will she love us ?"

I knew his feeling exactly! As an adult, I might be embarrassed to put it as simply and openly as he had, but the cry of the human heart is the same: "I want to be loved."

Knowing this so well then, Heavenly Father, why do I have so much trouble with it? Knowing Your command to love others, why should it be so hard? Would You command us to do something impossible?

And as I searched, I began finding some answers.

First came Johnny. He's the one with the cowlick and the runny nose. I can sympathize with anyone who has an allergy, but must he wipe it always on his shirt sleeve? He comes equipped with a rasping, whiny voice. He also has a habit of demanding attention. Love him?

Back I went running to the Word of God. What about John 3:16? "For God so loved the world" . . . that certainly seems to include Johnny. Then I found I John 4:11. "Beloved, if God so loved us, we ought also to love one another." *All right, then, Master, I need Your help.*

At a later date, it was a neighbor. You would have recognized her, too. She always came at the wrong time and stayed too long. She rambled on and on. Her kids were impossible.

Love her? How about that! She seems to be included also in John 3:16 and I John 4:11. Hmmm . . . I keep getting the same answers.

Then came one nobody could miss. A sister in Christ — blessed with perfect judgment and insight in all matters. I need say no more. You've all known one like her at some time. This assignment was even more difficult. Love her? Same answers!

Well, O.K., then, Father, but this time I desperately need Your help. Not instantly, but steadily as I have leaned on You, You have helped me grow in love. Seen through Your heart of love, the whining Johnnys and difficult neighbors and impossible saints become possible.

When Johnny left at the end of the year, I honestly hated to see him go. As I thought about it, he hadn't really changed any. He walked out with nose still running and mouth still in gear. *But You had changed me, Master. I couldn't have done it myself. You gave me Your love for him, and it became fun loving him for You.*

The neighbor was harder yet. And my fellow Christian the hardest of all. *But Your love was there, and I found You faithful. Sometimes I was a slow learner, but Your Holy Spirit was a patient teacher. And I'm still learning and growing. I know now I can come to You for help. And You will take my heart and make impossible things come true.*

National Love Week! At times I haven't seen much worth loving and felt greatly inclined not to do so. I am remembering that my forced, artificial smiles simply will not suffice for the deep needs of human hearts.

Keep Your love flowing through me, the kind that really fulfills the spirit of the law. Let me not forget I John 3:18: "My little children, let us love not in word, neither in tongue; but in deed and in truth."

HOW TO COPE WITH CORK GUNS

Chapter Thirteen

I am tired of coping.

Yesterday, I contended all day with a three-year-old on the eve of his becoming four. He was excited about his birthday celebration coming up later in the day. Any mother knows what that means — too much excitement to take a nap, plus a stream of incessant chatter.

He received some educational gifts and others of good quality. Naturally, he liked the present from his two brothers best. They (the same general variety of human beings) knew exactly what to get him — a pair of handcuffs and a cork gun!

After getting hit five times with a cork, I was ready to run said cork gun through the meat grinder. Now, some twenty-four hours later, the birthday excitement still has not abated.

To make life more interesting, today was also report card day. An intelligent son brought in a report card representing several degrees less than his best. This same intelligent son also placed a bottle of his model glue on his bed. This glue is the super-hold, quick-drying variety and almost instantly glued a section of the bedspread to the sheet. There was no hope except to cut a circle out of the bedspread.

We also remembered at the last hour before bedtime that the Halloween costumes had to be finished the next day.

Yes, I am tired of coping.

However, this was not the first attempt at coping, nor will it be my last. Over the years, I have been forced to develop some methods of dealing with such days. May you be blessed always with fair skies and sunny weather. But if storms should assail, perhaps my formula for coping will help.

1. If you must cry, do so; but not for long. For years, I labored under the delusion that a Christian mother should never admit frustration. Then I discovered that admitting I was still human sometimes helped. Too many tears may bring self-pity, however. In learning to cope, you must avoid self-pity as you would the plague.

2. This next step hurts, and you may cry again. Recheck the entire situation to see if you were the cause of any of it. A lack of organization, maybe? Were there telltale signs that a poor report card might be developing? Yes, of course. We had even discussed the matter, but perhaps not enough. Earlier counseling and more prayer might have helped.

Did I know the Halloween costumes had to be

finished by a certain date? Naturally. I have endured enough Halloweens to recognize all the signs of the season. But many other urgent matters were clamoring for my attention, and I thought the costumes could wait.

I think the glue problem was not foreseeable and thus becomes one of those sad facts of life that must be accepted. He certainly didn't mean to glue his bedspread and sheet together. It makes for uncomfortable sleeping. I can do nothing except mend the bedspread and try to forget. There is no reason for wasting more energy fretting

3. Bring out the old adage "Count your blessings," dust it off, and use it. *O.K., Lord, here goes, and I sure hope I feel better after this.*

Thank You, Father, for a wonderful four-year-old son; for his feet that go pitter-patter constantly, for his mouth that goes chitter-chatter constantly. Thank You, oh, thank You, for he is more precious than life itself to me. And thank You, too, for the older sons. I praise You for their keen minds, healthy bodies, their wit — and their love. There are so many happy days, when they do happy things, that I nearly have to sit on my hands to keep from clapping for them. Ah, yes, I feel much better already.

4. Learn to identify your rights, and appropriate the power available to you as a child of Jesus Christ.

"I can do all things through Christ which strengtheneth me" (Philippians 4:13).

"My God shall supply all your need according

to his riches in glory by Christ Jesus" (Philippians 4:19).

"Thy shoes shall be iron and brass; and as thy days, so shall thy strength be" (Deuteronomy 33:25).

These are not empty promises. Claim them by faith and place your confidence in the Almighty God. These words are bread and meat for weary mothers. The power of the Holy Spirit is available to get you through.

5. Remember, too, that no matter how troublesome the situation is, your response to the situation is the element that either makes or breaks the trial. Ask God for the correct response.

There you have it! My formula for coping. It works for all the copes — again . . . and again . . . and again . . . and again.

Lord, until we reach heaven, where coping will be no problem, help us face each new morning with courage and confidence in You. Cleanse us of self-pity and teach us to quit keeping such meticulous count of our trials. Let us count Your mercies instead as we continue to cope.

WAIT!

Chapter Fourteen

"If I manage to wait until this birthday, it will be a miracle," commented my oldest son, who was eagerly awaiting his special day. The prospect of getting a working model of a revolutionary new engine was making the moments drag by very slowly. He is not a good waiter.

Neither is his mother. I pace the floor. I wring my hands. I go over all the possible results again and again in my mind.

As a child, I rummaged every closet in the house before Christmas. Mother learned early never to share with me the secret of the family's gift to Daddy. I would promptly go and tell him what his present was, acting on the theory that he would not want to wait either.

I am not good at waiting in stations or at doctors' offices. I "read" a sixty-seven-page magazine in thirteen seconds. I then look around quickly to see whether anyone is staging an act of any sort. If not, I read another magazine in thirteen seconds. Then I get up and walk around. I may get a drink if a fountain is available. Then I blow my nose, whether I have a cold or not. Then I read another magazine, then I look around, then I get up and walk around, then I get a drink, then I blow my nose. Then . . . .

I have found the Holy Spirit to be an ever-faithful teacher. Just as I am patting myself on the back for some slight character improvement and settling down for a long rest, the Spirit insists on disturbing the status quo, and here we go again.

Lately, He has been speaking to me about waiting. I decided to research the word in a concordance. I stand dumbfounded at the spiritual results to be gained from learning to wait, and I am excited about starting the lessons. (In fact, I find myself wanting to learn how to wait *right now!)*

I find that there is spiritual strength to be gained from waiting patiently and expectantly. "Wait on the Lord: be of good courage, and he shall strengthen thine heart" (Psalm 27:14).

"But they that wait upon the Lord shall renew their strength; they shall mount up with wings as eagles; they shall run, and not be weary; and they shall walk, and not faint" (Isaiah 40:31.)

Would you like to inherit the earth? Learn to wait! "Evildoers shall be cut off: but those that wait upon the Lord, they shall inherit the earth" (Psalm 37:9).

I believe that waiting is also needful many

times as a period of preparation for what is to come. Galatians 4:4 tells us, "But when the fulness of time was come, God sent forth his Son." We know that God had spent many centuries preparing the world for this great event.

Waiting brings great blessing, and often, the longer the waiting, the sweeter the victory.

"The Lord is good unto them that wait for him, to the soul that seeketh him" (Lamentations 3:25). My father made his personal commitment to Christ at the age of sixty-four — just one year before his death. We had been praying for decades. The joy was almost unbearable when the news came of his decision. Also I found that my faith was greatly increased. I suppose the lesson might not have been so effective if we had been waiting only a few short days or weeks.

Those that wait need not be ashamed. "And thou shalt know that I am the Lord: for they shall not be ashamed that wait for me" (Isaiah 49:23).

Waiting helps bring about patience. If you have been praying for patience, watch out! You may be in for a long wait. "But if we hope for that we see not, then do we with patience wait for it" (Romans 8:25).

Then I found a thought that had not occurred to me before. Waiting may bring you new vision. "For the vision is yet for an appointed time, but at the end it shall speak, and not lie: though it tarry, wait for it; because it will surely come" (Habakkuk 2:3).

Perhaps the most thrilling result of waiting is that we shall eventually see what God has prepared for us. "For since the beginning of the world men have not heard, nor perceived by the ear, neither hath the eye seen, O God, beside thee, what he hath prepared for him that waiteth for him" (Isaiah 64:4).

Teach us, O Lord, to wait on Thee.

APPLEBY:
MAN
OF THE HOUR

Chapter Fifteen

"And he changeth the times and the seasons" (Daniel 2:21). As I write this, I have just finished ringing out an old year and have welcomed the new one. On further thought, I believe God actually ushers the years in and out. We simply go along with the idea and, indeed, are helpless to stop the hands of time. On such occasions, thoughts easily turn to the subject of time.

Perhaps because of the low density of the cells in my brain, my profound observations come very slowly. After celebrating some thirty-odd New Years' Days, however, I have learned a few things about time.

Time is no respecter of persons. The busiest world leader has not one second more or less than I do in each day. A New York socialite, a New Guinea savage, an Arab, and an Israeli each enjoys twenty-four hours daily, with sixty minutes to the hour.

No matter how rushed you consider yourself,

you have every whit as much time in your day as does your most relaxed acquaintance. However, we do not choose the number of days we shall live. We choose only whether to live each day fully.

Time is also fleeting. "Man is like to vanity; his days are as a shadow that passeth away" (Psalm 144:4). Time is easily wasted and is irretrievable. The New Testament speaks twice of "redeeming the time." (See Ephesians 5:16 and Colossians 4:5.)

How does one redeem time? Simply by turning each minute over to God in complete obedience to His leadership.

Time is an awesome and precious gift of God. This area of our lives should be approached with serious stewardship. Have you asked God to reveal to you the wisest use of your time?

Another conclusion I have reached: time can and should be measured by quality as well as quantity.

To the delight of my three sons, the second day of this new year was greeted by a six-inch snow. Great glittering flakes of gossamer floated steadily down in spectacular splendor. The sparkling backdrop was irresistible for a day of winter fun.

Only the ordinary business of life hindered me. I had just spent two weeks trying to keep the ceiling attached to the house during all the excitement of the Christmas holidays and school vacation.

Now decorations needed to be taken down.

Thank-you notes cried out to be written. The play area seemed to be in the terminal stages of disorder. And drastic steps needed to be taken to make the kitchen recognizable.

I am beginning to learn, however, about the quality of time. Eleven-year-olds turn twelve while you are popping a cake into the oven. Eight-year-olds turn nine while you are still wondering where the seventh year went. Four-year-olds go with madcap speed from babyish babbling to reading.

The domestic work could wait. The snow could not. I joined the boys outdoors.

We made snow angels. We threw snowballs. We went sledding. Then we built a lordly cross-eyed snowman and named him Bertram Appleby. He had walnut buttons and arms of dried chrysanthemum stalks.

In some future year, I will gaze with ineffable longing at the photograph I snapped of a small boy standing joyously by the side of Lord Appleby — and I will shake my head in wonder and say to myself as mothers have always done, "Where did the years go?" "What causes little boys to become men so quickly?" And I will remember this and other quality times, while an understanding of the quantity still eludes me.

Have you found the time lately to:
Smell honeysuckle?
Help a small child dig fishing worms?
Read a good book?
Pay an unexpected compliment to your spouse?

Get acquainted with a teenager?

Pray for a national or state leader by name?

Create a special memory for someone?

Listen to God?

"But I trusted in thee, O Lord: I said, Thou art my God. My times are in thy hand" (Psalm 31:14, 15a).

Heavenly Father, I pray that our time might become quality time as we commit all our days into Your loving hands.

GREAT
GLOBS
OF PAINT

Chapter Sixteen

I was painting the bedroom. Several problems had arisen. First, we had picked an off-white color to cover a dark green room which was now requiring three and four coats of paint. Then, each day as I prepared to paint, I kept getting calls to do substitute teaching, and I had been trying to paint that bedroom for some two weeks.

Finally, a day came when all else was pushed aside, and I prepared to spend the entire day painting.

Daylon, my three-year-old, was a ready and willing helper. The two boys who were old enough to really help naturally had urgent business elsewhere.

I grabbed a roll of masking tape and began taping some woodwork. Intent on my business, I paid no attention to the little boy puttering around behind my back. After a few minutes, I heard a swishing sound that caused me to look around.

Daylon in his great eagerness had decided to

start painting without me. He had drenched the paintbrush with paint and carried it across my woven rug to paint the opposite wall. He was now busily engaged with smearing paint in great globs as it ran all down his arms, over his clothes, and onto the rug.

Sharp words brought tears immediately.

I repented, cleaned up the mess, and then offered to help him with the painting. First, you may be sure we discussed the amount of paint that should be on a paintbrush. Then with my strong hand guiding his, we painted a few stripes until he was satisfied and ran off to play.

He was immensely pleased with himself and made a series of running comments.

"Mommy, see what a big boy I am to paint like this."

"Mommy, this looks very pretty, doesn't it?"

"Mommy, we are very, very good for our ages, aren't we?"

As I spent the next few hours listening to the humdrum swooshing of the paint roller up and down the wall I thought about that little incident.

I was appalled to remember the many times I had acted the part of a three-year-old spiritually, long after I should have reached maturity. How many times in my eagerness to show what I could do, I had grabbed a figurative paintbrush and headed off to pretty up the world, without waiting for the proper instructions.

I thought how often when the project had bogged down and I was standing in the middle of the mess, my Lord would say, "Now let's try it my way. Let me put my strong hand over yours and guide you." And with His powerful arm providing the necessary strength, the job had been done quickly and well.

I remembered especially my earlier years of marriage when I was trying to establish and care for a home and two preschoolers, teach school, and handle a half-dozen projects at church as well. I had enthusiastically tackled more jobs than two efficient people could do well. I had spread myself so thin I could not possibly do any of the jobs with Christian excellence. But I went right on "slopping the paint" and, in general, getting very spotty results.

Sometimes we Christians have a tendency to childish ways after God arrives on the scene and bails us out. Then we stand back and cast admiring glances and say to ourselves, "My, my, we are very good for our ages."

Our Father is patient with us. He often takes our efforts and from them makes something quite attractive. But how much better off we might have been to seek His will first, receive His instructions, and accept His way as best.

"So he fed them according to the integrity of his heart; and guided them by the skilfulness of his hands" (Psalm 78:72).

Lord God of all heaven, we want to be Your willing workers, but let us not rush ahead of You. And when we have at last begun the job under Your direction, put Your strong hands on ours and guide us so that the work accomplished will bring glory to Your own holy name.

WHOSE FAULT?

Chapter Seventeen

"Well, it was *your* responsibility."

"It was not, and you know it. It was *your* responsibility, and you didn't do it, and now you got me in trouble with Daddy."

"I still say it was *your* responsibility."

Responsibility! What a big word in more ways than length, and my sons were having problems with it. I was almost tempted to laugh until my thoughts drifted to the more serious side of the matter.

My boys still have a lot to learn about accepting responsibility. I suspect they are not alone with their problem.

Our society today does not help. Crimes are quickly blamed onto a bad environment. Illiteracy is easily traced back to a faulty school system. Never, but never, think that a grown boy reading at third-grade level may simply have goofed his merry way through twelve years of school.

A person may gain a goodly number of

sympathizers by crediting his lack of a well-rounded education to a faulty cultural heritage. In fact, such passing of the buck helps prevent the necessity of trips to the library to round out one's education. After the long drive to the library, then one must go to the trouble of reading the book and returning it. See how much simpler it is just to blame the family background.

Now they tell us that national no-fault car insurance is just around the corner. Thus, we are cleverly relieved of the need to be conscientious drivers (if we don't mind a few bumps and bruises of our own).

Just lately, I heard the story of two young law students. They were discussing their financial problems. One said to the other, "Oh, well, you need not worry about it. Just get married and let your wife work you through."

This tendency to evade responsibility must be contagious. Here I sit at the typewriter trying to blame my own troubled conscience on the attitude of society as a whole.

Let's see, now. To examine the matter more personally, another election day has passed into history. I truly meant to read up on the candidates and research the issues thoroughly this time. But the daily routine kept consuming my time, and anyway, hardly anyone else knew how or why he was voting either.

I stepped into the voting booth. A few names I had heard of with some vague labels floated around in my mind. On those, I voted according to labels.

One of the referendums was particularly well written (in fact, quite poetic). I liked the language and voted aye. For most of the rest, some straws or daisy petals would have been helpful in choosing.

Before you write me off as irresponsible, name three sound reasons that you chose the senator you did and make them specific, please. My brain gets muddled with words like *conservative* and *liberal.*

I also accepted a position on the music committee at church this year. A small responsibility, I told myself. However, the job does involve the inevitable committee meetings. I wonder whether it would matter much if I cheated a little on attendance. If you are a Sunday school teacher, how many workers' meetings have you attended this year?

I gained four pounds last month. I wonder who was responsibe for that? Actually, an unfulfilled subconscious desire from early child-hood drives me to the refrigerator. Or could it be merely that I am a weak-willed jellyfish who loves to eat?

I have honestly tried to examine some of the ecological issues of the day. I believe that Christians are in a special way caretakers of this planet God has given us. However, one day last week I got so cold I just couldn't take it anymore. I sneaked the thermostat from 68 back up to 72. After I was thoroughly warmed, I felt guilty and turned it back down.

What does God say about responsibility? I

remember the story about Jesus and the five foolish virgins who didn't keep their lights burning. I recall Jesus rebuking a faithless steward who did not use his talent responsibly.

I read in Romans 14:12, "So then every one of us shall give account of himself to God."

The simplicity and finality of that verse is stunning. A few exceptions would make it so much more palatable, except for political matters, except for ecological issues, except for a few personal hang-ups.

Ah, well, it's back to the old drawing board for me. I need to become a better steward; in short, I need to become more responsible. Will you join me?

Well, Lord, it's me again. Thank You for not giving up hope.

THE PERFECT WORD

Chapter Eighteen

I have had a lifelong love affair with words.

Some of my earliest memories include my father's glee when he discovered that at the age of three, I was already interested in letters and their sounds. He immediately taught me to spell *diphtheria* (that being the hardest word he could think of at the moment). From that time on, until I started to school, I was called forward at every family get-together to display my high intelligence by spelling diphtheria. I loved every minute of it.

From the first exciting moment when I discovered that letters make words and that words make ideas, no one could stop me from learning how to read.

In my enjoyment of our language, I have often asked groups of children about their favorite words. They generally start out with lighthearted suggestions, like "candy," "bicycle," or maybe "party." One little girl even nominated "barefoot."

They then became more philosophical, coming up with such goodies as "mother," "love," and "happiness." Occasionally, among children with a Christian background, some bright-eyed little ponytail will shyly speak up, "Jesus."

As a writer, I have discovered the familiar frustration of not being able to find exactly the right word. A word may have ten different meanings. Then each meaning may have its own little nuances, with various connotations to different people. Though we search and search, we wind up settling for some word slightly less than perfect.

God spoke once using the perfect Word, the "beginning and end" Word, the Word above all other words.

"In the beginning was the Word, and the Word was with God, and the Word was God. The same was in the beginning with God. All things were made by him; and without him was not any thing made that was made. In him was life; and the life was the light of men" (John 1:1-4).

That Word, of course, was Jesus. He is the Word, the Life, the Light. And, oh, what a Word!

A royal Word, residing in a cattle shed, sleeping on hay in a manger.

A healing Word, touching blind eyes and deformed limbs, making crippled bodies whole again.

A restoring Word, clothing the demonic with his reason once more.

A powerful Word, feeding five thousand with only five loaves and two fishes.

A compassionate Word, crying over the death

of a friend; and a living Word, restoring life to that same friend.

A Word of pardon, saying, "Arise and walk. Thy sins be forgiven thee."

A joyful Word, "These things have I spoken unto you, that my joy might remain in you, and that your joy might be full."

People loved that Word and praised it, waving palm leaves with hosannas ringing.

Then something happened. The mood of the crowd changed. Someone spoke accusing words. And this perfect Word was brought into court on false charges. People thought they could rid the world of this Word. They mocked Him. They spit upon Him. They crowned Him with thorns.

They nailed God's divine Word to the tree. This Word still spoke, saying incomprehensible things like "Forgive them, Father, for they know not what they do."

The dead Word was taken from the cross and placed in a dark cave. Some clapped their hands with glee. Many shrugged their shoulders and said, "There. That's that! We'll hear that Word no more."

Then the great discovery came. That Word could not be shushed by pounding nails through its hands and feet. That Word could not be quieted by stabbing it through with a spear. That Word could not be deleted from the world's language by sealing it inside a tomb.

The Word rose from the tomb, is alive, and is even now preparing a place in heaven for you and me.

This precious Word has spoken down through the centuries since that time. Disciples have followed this Word, many at great cost. Tens of thousands of hymns and poems have been dedicated to telling the world of this Word. Martyrs step forth and gladly offer up their lives for this Word.

This Word still speaks today. It means love, joy, peace. This Word is identified as Saviour and giver of eternal life.

Thank you, God, for Your Word,
  the final Word,
    the living Word,
      the perfect Word.
Thank You for Jesus.

KEEP ON
KEEPING ON

Chapter Nineteen

The book was wordy and obtuse. The young woman made several starts and an equal number of stops. She simply could not wade through. The book held no interest for her. She pushed the volume back on the shelf, and dust collected.

Some months later, the young girl attended a party. To her great surprise, she met there the author of the book. He was a very dashing young man, highly intelligent, sensitive, and handsome. She could hardly wait to get home and read the book.

This time the book held her interest. In fact, she could hardly put it down before the end. The difference? She had fallen in love with the author.

While working my way through college, I had trouble finding time to read and study the Bible personally. I made excuses. I was, after all, attending a Christian college and taking courses of study from the Bible. Why should I try to find the time to have personal devotions?

After college, and when teaching school full time, I again was startled to discover that I had no real interest in studying the Bible deeply for myself. I wondered what was wrong. Then I heard the above story.

I had to face the fact that my love for the real Author of the Book might have become luke-warm.

I then embarked upon a program to establish a personal devotional life that would promote my own spiritual maturity. Since that time, I have had periodic struggles in being consistent. I still have busy days when Bible study and prayer seem an added chore. However, the Lord has helped me develop a rewarding life that contributes to my Christian growth. I would like to share with you just a few points that have helped me.

1. As I stated earlier, you must keep a fresh and personal relationship with the Author. A fading desire to read the Bible often indicates a waning interest in God and His affairs.

When I was home for the summer after my freshman year of college, my boyfriend occasion-ally wrote to me. I would often pick up his letter disinterestedly from the mailbox and with a big "ho-hum," stick it into my pocket, sometimes forgetting to read it for days.

Do you believe that?

If you don't, my mother will agree with you. She knows. I could not even wait to get back to the house. I read the letter on the spot with great enthusiasm. I then walked back into the house and reread it before I returned to my chores. As soon as I deserved a break, I would often snatch the letter from its resting place and read it again. My interest in the young man who wrote the letter made every detail important to me. A warm and personal relationship with God should make His words attractive to you.

2. A busy woman in today's world must learn to say no. A thousand worthy causes cry out to be served. For volunteer work we are almost indispensable. We are hounded on all sides to improve ourselves by studying French cooking or by enrolling at some reducing salon. We have opportunities to take adult classes in accounting, batik, classical guitar — and so on down the list through Z.

I finally reached the point where I insisted on some time of my own. I knew I needed the spiritual power and peace of mind that comes from a daily time apart with the Master. One must simply learn to drop some worthy cause for a far worthier one. If you are too busy to have devotions, you are doing more work than God intended you to do. Ask God where you should say no.

3. Remember that your body, mind, and spirit all deserve some time for relaxation and meditation. I often felt guilty if I took an hour away from my work to sit down and do nothing. Jesus' words helped here: "And Mary hath chosen that good part" (Luke 10:42). Mary had chosen fellowship with the Master. Dinner could wait.

A time of rest with my Bible and prayer list

refresh me and enable me to face the rest of the day with renewed strength. The busy work then gets done more enthusiastically. I also discovered that this helped me to organize the rest of my day more effectively.

4. Minimize the distractions. Note I did not say *avoid* all distractions. A busy homemaker might spend several years waiting for an opportune time to have devotions. No, I said *minimize* the distractions.

This means you do not sit in the kitchen with the dirty dishes staring you in the face while you try to delve deeply into Romans 12. You organize your schedule to leave time while preschoolers are napping, or else beat them awake in the morning.

What distracts one person may not distract another. Observe yourself closely over a period of time. You will be able to discover the things that most often cause your mind to wander. Then figure out some shift of time or place that will take care of the problem.

Let's keep on keeping on! The enemy is real, and as long as we remain mortal he will be trying new ways to discourage us from studying God's message. Two words are helpful: discipline and determination. Determine before God, that the less you are feeling like being "spiritual," the more you will come to Him for encouragement. Then ask God to help you discipline your thoughts and bring them in line with His.

Lord God, thank You for wanting our fellowship. Thank You for offering Yours.

LET
FREEDOM
RING

Chapter Twenty

I have, at long last, finished reading Aleksandr Solzhenitsyn's *Gulag Archipelago,* Parts I and II. I discovered from the first few pages that this book was not one to be read rapidly or lightly. Thus, I have spent several weeks getting through the entire volume.

My reaction was typical of many: How does an entire nation allow itself to be so deceived? Perhaps it was not an entire nation — here and there a few perceived the coming bondage and tried to prevent it. But there were apparently not enough people who were willing to act positively. Or perhaps they did not know what to do. What could they have done? That question disturbs me.

Then the next question comes to mind: How do we keep the same type of thing from eventually occurring in our own country?

As a mother, the question has become more personal to me. What can I do for my children to insure that their generation will continue to enjoy the civil and religious liberties for which our nation has been so famous during the past two centuries?

I don't feel that I have any perfect answers, but these quotations from the book have started me thinking.

"We didn't love freedom enough. And even more — we had no awareness of the real situation" (p. 13).

"A person who is not inwardly prepared for the use of violence against him is always weaker than the person committing the violence" (p. 14).

"Every man always has handy a dozen glib little reasons why he is right not to sacrifice himself" (p. 17).

"However, the root destruction of religion in the country, which throughout the twenties and thirties was one of the most important goals of the GPU-NKVD, could be realized only by mass arrests of orthodox believers .... True, they were supposedly being arrested and tried not for their actual faith but for openly declaring their convictions and for bringing up their children in the same spirit .... A person convinced that he possessed spiritual truth was required to conceal it from his own children" (p. 37).

These statements shook me up! So I have begun to formulate my own "freedom" program.

1. I must teach my sons to love freedom — to cherish this precious gift above any other of their rights and privileges (except their own relationship with Christ).

2. I must set the example before my sons in

trying to be well informed about governmental and political matters which would really be easier to ignore. I must become actively involved in whatever small way possible in open, constructive government.

I must know my congressmen and their stands on political issues. I must consider voting day a true date with destiny. I must support all the worthwhile issues that I can. I dare not be caught unaware, for it will be the precious liberty of their generation slipping through my fingers.

3. I must keep constant "watchguard" over the development of their character. Pampered children with flabby spiritual muscles will not be able to stand in a desperate struggle against bondage. Children who have developed an almost total dependence on material possessions will be lacking the moral courage — the sacrificial brand of stamina — necessary to wage a battle of intangible values.

4. I must (and as a mother, oh, how this one hurts) teach them at least a dozen reasons why, if necessary, they *should* be willing to sacrifice themselves for a world in which individual humans have the right to maintain their personal freedoms.

5. I must not merely live and let live, but I must actively support as many truly spiritual and religious endeavors as is possible in one lifetime. When the churches become empty voluntarily, the people themselves have actually voted for the destruction of religion. Anyone asleep on Sunday mornings without illness has already voted.

Every spiritual impulse in my children must be fostered. Each action indicating a preference for the spiritual over the material must be encouraged. Every decision in our home must be made with eternal values in view. Our priorities must be set in favor of human personalities and against all philosophies that dehumanize man and make him become just another cog in the machinery of the state.

6. And last, I must spare no effort in communicating to my children my own personal relationship with Jesus Christ. Is it not strange that in America, where we are completely free in our homes to pass our religious heritage on to our children, we often, by volition or neglect, conceal it from them? Must we be faced with mass arrests before this privilege becomes precious enough that we will begin to exercise it?

God of true freedom, keep us free as we consider our own responsibilities – the other side of the coin of liberty. And thank You for the freedom of spirit that comes only by knowing Jesus Christ.

Quotations from *Gulag Archipelago, Part I,* Aleksandr Solzhenitsyn, Harper & Row, Publishers, 1974. Used by permission.

HOW DO YOU SPELL JOY?

Chapter Twenty-one

Three-year-olds are sometimes becoming interested in the alphabet. Son Three is just now reaching this stage. All his favorite words must be spelled out to him several times each day. In the middle of a conversation, he interrupts with a "Mommy, how do you spell _____?" naming some fascinating word he has just heard.

This son also loves music, and several times each day we stop long enough to sing a favorite chorus of his. One day last week we rested amid our day's activities. We were giving forth a very hearty rendition of "I Have the Joy, Joy, Joy, Joy down in My Heart" when he stopped to ask, "Mommy, how do you spell *joy?*"

I spelled *joy* L-A-U-G-H-T-E-R this week. I pulled a good joke on your daddy — a wholesome, funny one. He had been asking for it for a long time, and we have both been chuckling since. Love and laughter seem to go together and can easily spell *joy.*

Joy was spelled with A-C-H-I-E-V-E-M-E-N-T

this week. Hardly anything matches the good feeling of accomplishment when a hard task is finished and we hear God say, "Well done."

I finished writing another chapter. I baked some cookies that were greatly appreciated. I prepared my Sunday school lesson well in advance. And I washed some windows which definitely gave me a brighter outlook on the world. In a way I can hardly explain, each of these small chores added purpose and meaning to my life.

The chapter written was a chance for me to share my heart's thoughts with another. The cookies were a good opportunity to prove that I keep my word (for I had promised them several days before). Bright windows seem to say that a home is important to its occupants. And that Sunday school lesson may touch some child's heart and life.

You, my boy child, are already learning this sense of satisfaction and joy. Just a few days ago, I instructed you to pick up in your room. You hummed around like a little bee as you moved toys from here to there, stuffed clothes crazily into drawers, and shuffled books around from one shelf to another. After a few minutes, you emerged from the room, clapped your hands together with delight, and said, "There, now. I am a very, very good boy!" And life was sweet to you.

May you always be able to spell *joy* in your life through doing God's work cheerfully and with excellence.

I also spelled *joy* this week with the letters B-O-O-K. I found an especially good one, the kind that will not be set aside. God spoke from the pages directly to my heart, and I felt myself growing in spirit. Yes, little boy, if I can teach you a love for reading good literature, books will always be counted among your best friends. They will enrich your life and feed your soul. And do not ever forget, the best of all possible literature is found in the Bible, the one Book that speaks with God's mouth.

The easiest way I know to spell *joy* is J-E-S-U-S. My son, take Him with you wherever you go, and He will forever spell *joy* for you.

"I will rejoice in the Lord, I will joy in the God of my salvation" (Habakkuk 3:18).

Lord, I thank You today for the gift of emotions. Yes, sometimes I misuse them, but with them I experience Your love, peace, and joy. Thank You for my eyes, with which I see Your joyful world. Thank You for my mouth, with which I can tell and sing of joy. And thank You for my mind, with which I claim Your promise of joy. Accept my joy today as a shining gift of praise to You.

HE GAVE HIMSELF AWAY

Chapter Twenty-two

He is only four and still thinks the world revolves around himself. His older brothers had crossed him, and he was crushed. Then he became angry.

He came stomping through the living room with tears streaming down his face. When my youngest son saw me, he immediately beseeched my aid in helping him get his own way. When I refused, he shook an impertinent fist and declared with great emphasis, "Well, all right then. I'll just go give myself away!"

A little firmness was obviously needed at that point, and I tried hard to hide my smile. Later, in private, my husband and I were greatly amused. Little did that little boy realize the enormity of his threat. If he had carried through with it, a great source of delightful sunshine would have been removed from our lives.

As so often happens with children, however, his remark later gave me occasion for thinking.

And a picture came to my mind.

I could see Jesus, high and lifted up — seated on a heavenly throne beside His Father.

He arose and looked down upon planet earth. There He saw us — helpless mites that we are — racing around in turmoil and strife; a human race of sinners, one and all; lost, frightened, confused — totally unworthy. We were headed for doom with no hand to stay us. His great heart swelled with compassion.

He moved a step forward with tears streaming down His face. But these were not tears of anger. They flowed with loving mercy. He moved farther away from the breathtaking splendor of heaven. As His steps led closer and closer to earth, I could hear Him say, "Yes, I'll just go give myself away."

He was born in obscurity and had to flee His native country at an early age. Even after He returned and worked miracles, His own home folks could not believe. (See Matthew 13:52-57.) But He persisted in His purpose, for He had come to give himself away.

He was sold for thirty pieces of silver by a man who later threw the money down and hanged himself in guilt.

He was accused falsely in court and answered not one word in self-defense. (See Matthew 27:12-14.) It didn't really matter much what they said, since He had come to give himself away.

As the strong cords of love held Him fast to the cross, He asked forgiveness for His murderers. He offered salvation to a dying thief. As the racking pain ravaged His body, He could have ordered a legion of angels to free Him. But He didn't. He had come to give himself away.

The load of humanity's sin grew heavier. Finally, the sight of all that sin grew so intolerable, the Father himself turned His back. Jesus could have stepped down off that cross and left the terrible agony behind, but He didn't. Oh, praise God, He didn't. He was giving himself away — for you and me.

He gave the supreme gift — eternal life.

And wonderful truth: this offering up of himself was free and available to all, free for the asking, available to any person of any creed or color who would come in repentance and belief, accepting the sacrifice on the cross for his own personal salvation.

"Thanks be unto God for his unspeakable gift" (II Corinthians 9:15).

Yes, thank You, Jesus, for giving yourself for me. If there be even one reader who has not yet seen You in Your most glorious hour – when You gave yourself away – lead him even now to the foot of the cross. Help him accept the Giver of the most wonderful gift – eternal life through Jesus Christ, our Lord.